Benjamin~
we are very proud and
happy to be your Godparents
today!

Love
Auntie Christy
and
Uncle Jim

P9-CER-304

Today I Was Baptized

Revised Edition

Written by Dianne Ahern   Illustrated by Bill Shurtliff

Aunt Dee's Attic, Inc.

Today I Was Baptized © 2009 Aunt Dee's Attic

A Book from Aunt Dee's Attic

PUBLISHED BY

Aunt Dee's Attic
415 Detroit Street, Suite 200
Ann Arbor, MI 48104

Printed and bound in Canada by Friesens

All rights reserved

All materials in this publication, including illustrations, are protected by copyright laws. No reproductions, either by printed or electronic means, may be made in any form without specific written permission from the copyright holders.

Library of Congress Number: 2009900367

ISBN-13: 978-0-9679437-5-6

1 2 3 4 5 6 7 8 9 10

Revised Edition

www.auntdeesattic.com

Printed with Ecclesiastical Permission. Most Reverend Earl Boyea. September 15, 2008

RESCRIPT

In accord with canon 827, S3 of the *Code of Canon Law,* I hereby grant my permission to publish the revised edition of

Today I Was Baptized
by Dianne Ahern

The work is an illustrated guide to baptism. Notice of this rescript is to be printed on the reverse side of the title page of the booklet.

Given in the Curia of the Diocese of Lansing on this the 5th day of February, 2009, the Memorial of Saint Agatha.

Most Reverend Earl Boyea
Bishop of Lansing

Dedication

This book is dedicated to Father Roger Prokop who has been an inspiration, spiritual advisor, contributor, coach, critic, and good friend during the development of Aunt Dee's Attic.

Acknowledgements

A very special thank you to all the people who assisted the author and illustrator in making this book possible, in particular:

- The staff of Saint Thomas the Apostle Church, Ann Arbor; especially Father Jeffrey Njus, Father Charles Canoy, Cathy Smalley, Karmen Saran, Timothy Carpenter, and Tony Moskus

- Janet Shurtliff, Bill's wife and collaborator

- Josiah and Emily Shurtliff and their children Evelyn and John

- Gregory and Keenan Allion and their daughter Helen

- Jillian Downey who provided the text design and layout

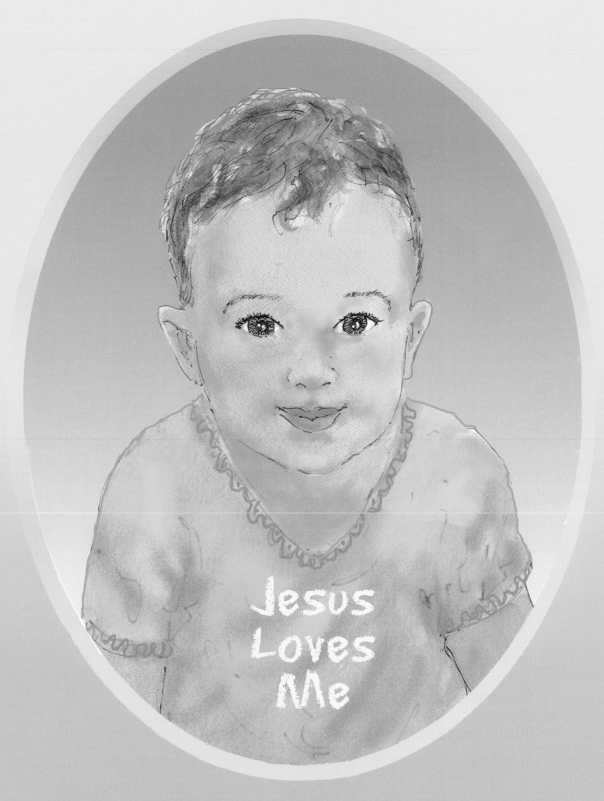

Jesus
Loves
Me

I knew immediately when I awoke this morning
that today would be a special day.

You see, my Mom was excited about something and during my bath we did a lot more "cooing" and "wooing" to each other than usual.

Already I have learned to tell from the tone of her voice what will be an ordinary day and what will be a special day.

In fact, the entire house is filled with excitement.
Everybody is "getting ready" for something.
SOMETHING SPECIAL!

On my dressing table I can see that in place of my comfy play clothes lays the most beautiful white gown I have ever seen.

"Is that for me!?" I want to shout.

S ure enough, as soon as everyone else has on their dress-up clothes, Mom and Dad begin putting the beautiful white gown on me.

I squirm and giggle and wiggle. Mom and Dad tug and hug.

There, it is finally on me.

WOW, I look like an angel!

We all get in the car and off we go to a place called "church." The "church" is big, with more people inside than I have ever seen.

The light coming through the windows puts rainbows on the faces and places.

Up in front, there is a big man. "Look!" He has on a white gown and colorful robe. His clothes are almost as beautiful as mine.

The big man in the white gown and colorful robe smiles at me and touches my cheek. This is going to be OK!

"What do you want for this child today?" The big man in the white gown loudly, proudly asks my parents.

"Baptism," they reply.

"Are there sponsors or godparents?" He asks.

"I am the godmother," says the woman standing beside my Mom. "I am the godfather," says the man standing next to my Dad.

The big man in white asks my parents and godparents if they will love and guide me, help me to live a Christian life, to accept God's grace, and to resist and reject evil powers, injustices, and oppression. They say they will.

Just about the time I begin to fall asleep, the big man in white pours water over my head.

"**I baptize you** *in the name of the Father, and of the Son, and of the Holy Spirit,*" he says.

I make a funny face. This must be amusing because everybody smiles and giggles while I squirm and wiggle.

The big man in the beautiful robe turns to the people and says, *"Please welcome this new Christian and the newest member of our Church."*

The people cheer and clap their hands.
This is SPECIAL.

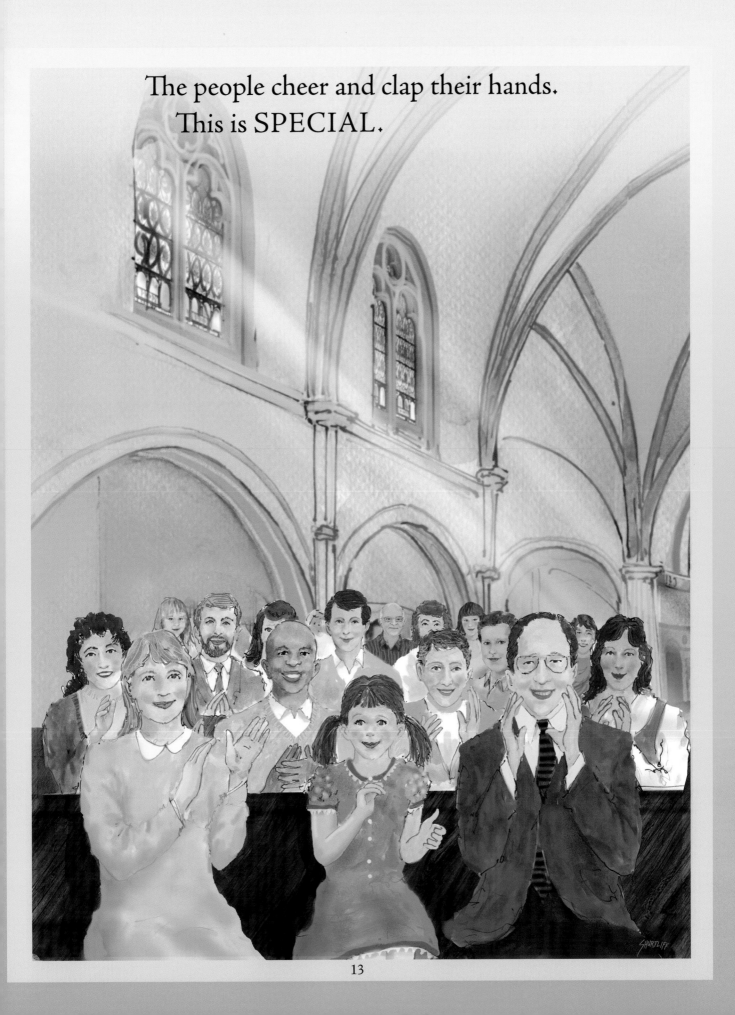

13

We all go home and there is a big celebration.
There is food and music, presents and lively conversation.
What a WONDERFUL and SPECIAL DAY!

My Mom and I go to my room where it is quiet. I could use a little nap, as this has been one very busy day. Mom and I sit in her rocking chair and she talks to me in her very special voice.

"My precious little one," she says. "Today we helped you to become a Christian. You received God's grace through Baptism. From now on God's grace and our love will help you to grow strong in faith and spirit."

We rock and "coo" and "woo" to each other.

As I drift off to sleep, I feel the flutter of little angel wings inside my soul.

You see,

TODAY IS A VERY SPECIAL DAY.
TODAY I WAS BAPTIZED.

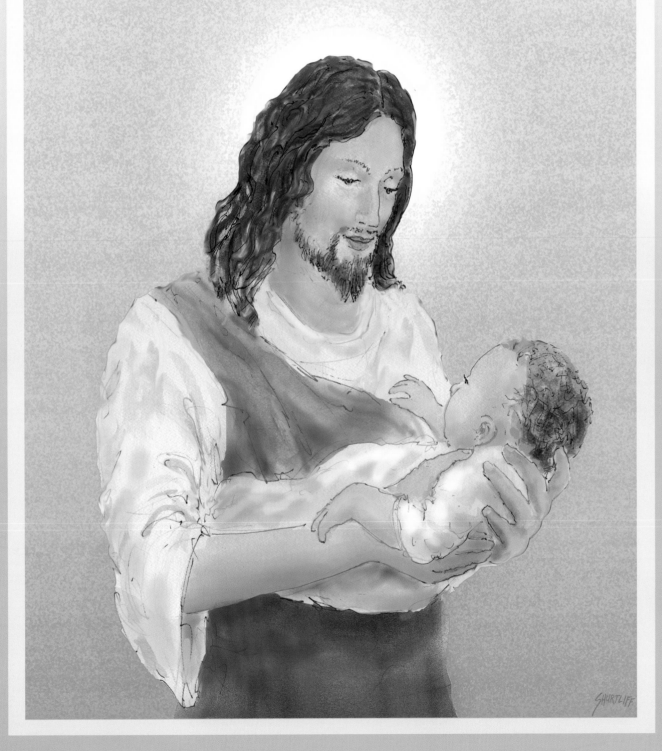

Short Essays on Baptism

Why We Baptize

Why and How We
Use Water In Baptism

The Baptism of
Jesus Christ

How Jesus Conferred
the Right to Baptize to
the Apostles

Anointing With Oil

The Baptismal Gown

Why We Baptize

Baptism is the sacrament of initiation and incorporation into the Body of Christ. Through Baptism, children born into the brokenness of the world receive the cleansing and renewing forgiveness of God, are recipients of His grace and love, become members of His Church, and receive an indelible mark necessary for salvation.

Most Christians believe there is a "spiritual disease" we all get just by being born into a world that is out-of-kilter. (We know the world is out-of-kilter because there are wars, family squabbles, and sometimes problems we have to deal with that we ourselves have not caused.) We call that spiritual disease, Original Sin.

In the beginning, after God made heaven and earth and all the animals, God made man and woman in his likeness. He gave them the most beautiful place to live. The man and woman were named Adam and Eve, and their home was called the Garden of Eden. God gave them something special, something He did not give to the plants and animals. He gave them the ability to speak, to think, and to make decisions. God trusted they would use this special ability to live rich and fruitful lives, to do good deeds, and to repel the powers of Satan.

God told Adam and Eve that they could have and do anything they wanted, except He forbid them to eat the fruit of one special tree. Then along came Satan in the form of a serpent. The serpent encouraged Eve, and she encouraged Adam, to eat the fruit of the forbidden tree. After all, what harm could it do? They could become like God!

Adam and Eve, having the God given ability to determine right from wrong, decided to follow the serpent's temptation anyway. When they thought God wasn't looking, they took and ate the forbidden fruit. This was against God's command; Adam and Eve knew it, but they did it anyway.

God did see Adam and Eve eat the forbidden fruit, and shamed them, saying, "You have sinned, not just for yourself, but for all of mankind." This spoiled it for the rest of us because, being descendants of Adam, we all inherited part of his sin, the Original Sin.

In His mercy, though, God gave us the Sacrament of Baptism to be used as an inoculation against the ravages of that spiritual disease called Original Sin. Baptism frees us of Original Sin *and* provides us with the grace of God and the strength of

His Church to live rich and fruitful lives. However, as with Adam and Eve, how we decide to live our lives is up to us.

We should note that the word Adam, in the Hebrew language, means "man" or "humankind." The Genesis story may not only be an account of how the world got out-of-kilter; it may also be a biography of you and me.

Why and How We Use Water In Baptism

Throughout all time, water has been characterized as being the source of life and fruitfulness, a source of death and destruction, and has the ability to cleanse and refresh.

- Water from hurricanes and floods destroy life and property
- Without water, rivers run dry and the fertile earth becomes desert
- Water that falls on the earth brings forth new foliage
- Water brings health and life to those who drink it

God's use of water is referenced in baptismal prayers:

When nothing existed but chaos, you swept across the dark waters and brought forth light.

In the days of Noah you saved those on the ark through water. After the flood you set in the clouds a rainbow.

When you saw your people as slaves in Egypt, you led them to freedom through the sea. Their children you brought through the Jordan to the land which you promised.

In the fullness of time you sent Jesus, nurtured in the water of a womb.

In Baptism, water is administered three times as the priest, deacon, or minister recites the words, "*N.,* I baptize you in the Name of the Father, and of the Son, and of the Holy Spirit."

The effects of the water are threefold: the water is administered to destroy or drown the sin that each of us is born with or has committed between the time of birth and baptism, the soul is cleansed and purified and the person is reborn, and he/she becomes a member of the Church, the mystical body of Christ. Through the Sacrament of Baptism, the person enters the Kingdom of God. He is saved.

Many Christian faiths perform baptism by pouring or sprinkling water over the head of the baptismal participant. Others practice baptism by immersion. The practice of immersion is believed to reflect the manner in which Christ was baptized. Although the form may differ, the effects of baptism are the same: the death of the sinful man, purification and rebirth, and becoming a member of the Church.

The Baptism of Jesus Christ

Did you know that Jesus Christ was baptized even though He was without sin? As Jesus approached adulthood and was about to go out into the world to begin his earthly ministry, he asked John the Baptist, who was one of His disciples, to baptize Him.

The baptismal rite that John was performing at the time was for repentance from and forgiveness of sin in preparation for the coming of the Kingdom of God. John was calling on people to confess and turn from their sins, and to show the fruit of their repentance by submitting to baptism. Baptism therefore was an outward sign of an inward work, one performed in anticipation of the coming of the Messiah.

That Jesus would ask to be baptized was surprising to John because he knew Jesus to be the Son of God, the true Messiah, and without sin.

When Jesus approached John, however, He made it clear that His baptism was not for the repentance of sin, but as an act of obedience to the Father. God said people must be baptized and Jesus followed His rules. Jesus was deliberately and consciously establishing a standard of behavior and setting an example for His disciples and others to follow.

Once Jesus was baptized, and as He came up from the water of the River Jordan, the heavens opened to Him and He saw the Spirit of God descending like a dove and alighting on him. A voice from heaven said, "This is my Son, the Beloved, with whom I am well pleased." (Matthew 3:13)

NOTE: The baptism for repentance of sin that John performed is different than the Christian baptism performed after Christ's death and resurrection. The Christian baptism is for the "washing" away of sin, not the repentance of sin. Christian baptism is a figure of death, burial, and resurrection of Christ and our being raised with Him.

2

How Jesus Conferred the
Right to Baptize to the Apostles

Jesus Christ instituted the Sacrament of Baptism through his Apostles. He not only commanded His Disciples to baptize and gave them the form to be used, but He also declared the absolute necessity of Baptism.

> *"Unless a man be born again of water and the Holy Spirit, he can not enter into the Kingdom of God." (John 3)*

> *During His ministry on earth, Jesus commissioned His disciples to baptize. (John 3-4:1,2)*

> *Jesus said to his disciples, "Go into all the world and preach the gospel to the whole creation. He who believes and is baptized will be saved; but he who does not believe will be condemned." (Mark, 16:15-16)*

> *When He was ready to ascend into heaven after His resurrection, His last command was "Go ye therefore, and teach all nations, baptizing them in the name of the Father, and of the Son, and of the Holy Spirit." (Matthew 28:19)*

Today, bishops, priests, deacons, and local pastors are the ministers of Baptism. The rite, passed down through the Apostles, is performed on both infants and adults, but it need be performed only once.

Under extraordinary conditions, when a person is in an emergency situation, is near death, and has not been baptized, baptism can be administered validly by any person who observes the essential conditions. The belief is that the unbaptized person should receive the Grace of God, have sins forgiven, and have the opportunity to enter the Kingdom of God. The person recognizing the emergency and fully comprehending the need and responsibility for baptism must pour water upon the one to be baptized and, at the same time, pronounce the words: *"I baptize you in the name of the Father, and of the Son, and of the Holy Spirit."*

Anointing With Oil

Some religions, most notably Catholic, anoint the infant/person with sacred chrism, perfumed oil, during the baptism ceremony. This signifies the gift of the Holy Spirit to the newly baptized, who has become a Christian, that is, one "anointed" by the Holy Spirit, incorporated into Christ who is the anointed priest, prophet, and king.

Christ means the "anointed" one. The infant/person following baptism is anointed and becomes "Christ-ed" or Christian.

The Baptismal Gown

The white gown or vestment worn for baptism reflects the purity of the soul following Baptism and that the person has risen with Christ.

The baptismal gown selection and preparation has become a special ritual in itself. Many families pass the baptismal gown down through generations. Others select a new gown for each child's baptism.

My Baptism Memories

My name is _____

My parents are _____

_____

My Godparents are _____

_____

Today is _____
and this is my Baptism day.

My Baptism took place at _____

_____

Officiating at my Baptism
was the Reverend _____

The Baptismal gown or outfit I wore today is (describe):

_____

_____

_____

_____

_____

My parents had a celebration following my Baptism, and it included (describe the celebration, what foods were served, special decorations and favors, unusual events of the day, etc.):

_____

_____

_____

_____

_____

_____

_____

_____

_____

_____

_____

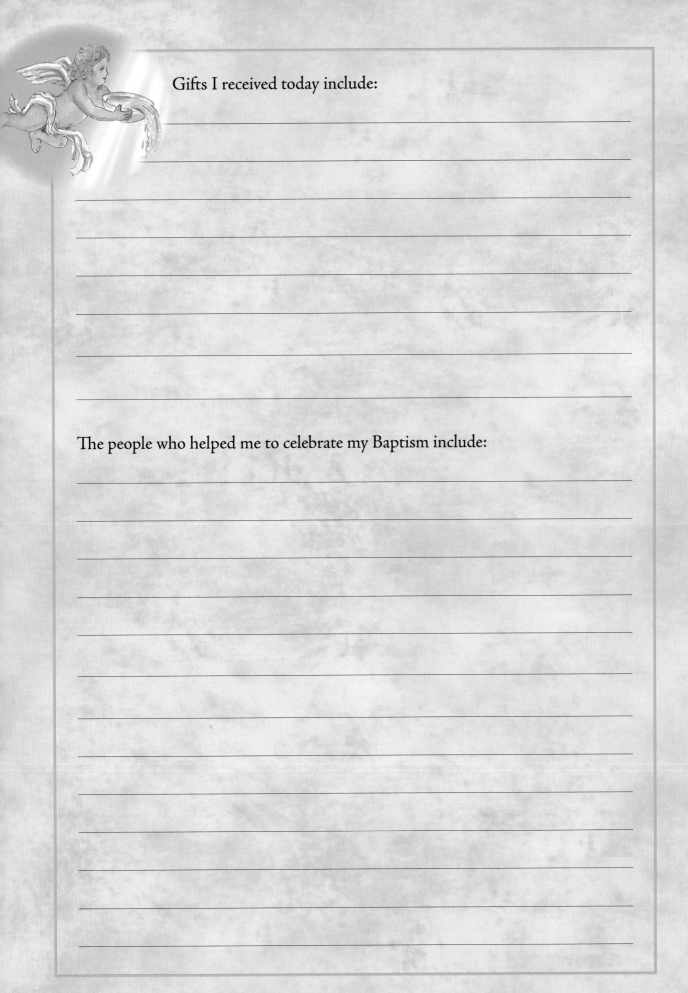

Gifts I received today include:

_____

_____

_____

_____

_____

_____

The people who helped me to celebrate my Baptism include:

_____

_____

_____

_____

_____

_____

_____

_____

_____

_____

_____

A Message from Mom on the Day of My Baptism:

_____

_____

_____

_____

_____

_____

_____

A Message from Dad on the Day of My Baptism:

_____

_____

_____

_____

_____

_____

_____

_____

_____

Messages from My Godparents, Sponsors, and Others on the Day of My Baptism:

_____

_____

_____

_____

_____

_____

_____

_____

_____

_____

_____

_____

_____

_____

_____

_____

_____

_____

_____

_____

Photographs and Souvenirs of My Baptism

Photographs and Souvenirs of My Baptism

Photographs and Souvenirs of My Baptism

Photographs and Souvenirs of My Baptism

Photographs and Souvenirs of My Baptism